Praise for ***transcena***

"Catalina Pietro's *transcend* is comfort food for the heartbroken, for those quiet moments of grief that ask for your stillness and reflection. The collection is easy to digest and will no doubt connect with anyone who has ever gone through a breakup."
— Maverick L. Malone, Author of *Pressed Petals*

"This book is for those who love with every fragment of the universe and hurt twice as much. A beautiful blend of truth, honesty, and emotion."
— Carrie A. White, Author of *Teeth of Eden*

"This collection is gorgeous and feels like a friend holding your hand as you travel through the emotions of acceptance and release. You can feel every word Prieto writes, like rain falling onto your head as you journey through each and every poem."
— Tiffiny Rose Allen, Author of *At The Beginning Of Yesterday*

"Whether it's your first heartbreak you're mourning or your last, Catalina Prieto's *transcend* is here to help you heal the hurt. It's here to help you emerge a more resilient version of yourself through the vulnerable power of words."
— Flor Ana, Author of *A Moth Fell In Love With The Moon*

"*transcend* is a duality of sensuality and stinging. It caresses you sweetly, and then forces you to think of each time you thought you were loved. Catalina Prieto paints a rose with her words, and then fortifies the thorns—a beautiful collection."
— John Queor, Author of *Resembling A Moth*

"Catalina Prieto's *transcend* smartly knits together what it feels like to candidly dive into love, drown in heartache, and triumphantly re-emerge floating with self-love."
— Annie Vazquez, Founder of *The Fashion Poet*

"Catalina Prieto expresses the weathering in our ever-changing hearts through her collection *transcend*, and the clarity that comes after the chaos. 'Allow the rain to seep into the crevices of your scars,' she says, 'Nurture your seeds, and allow yourself to blossom.'"
— Sarah Ciminillo, Author of *A Love in Lockdown*

"*transcend* is a stunning collection of poetry that takes you through the stages of grief. Catalina put words on a page that my mind has sought for during the periods of heartbreak. This is poetry that is beautifully true. transcend proves that our emotions are just as lovely when they are damaged."
— Kendall Hope, Author of *The Willow Weepings*

"Beautifully written, Catalina Prieto takes us on the path of being in love, falling out of love, heartbreak, and finding the love within. Reaching for self-love while going through the emotions to get there, this is a journey into the depths of the self. A powerful story of transcending all obstacles through self-love."
— Courtni A. Tansey, Author of *Ready to Evolve*

"In her debut poetry collection, Catalina Prieto delicately weaves together lessons in love, relationships, heartbreak, and healing into a beautiful tapestry of growth and transformation. Full of warmth and gentle wisdom, *transcend* provides encouragement and clarity for all hurting hearts as they emerge from the depths of healing into the arms of their own compassion, wholeness, and self-love."
— A.W. Jones, Starred Review

transcend

Catalina Prieto

Copyright © 2023 by Catalina Prieto

All rights reserved.

This book (or any portion thereof) may not be reproduced or used in any manner without written permission from the author except in the context of reviews.

Cover Art Copyright © 2023 by Indie Earth Publishing
Section Illustrations Copyright © 2023 by Indie Earth Publishing
Illustrations Curation by Indie Earth Publishing

Edited by Flor Ana Mireles

1st Edition | 01
Hardcover ISBN: 978-1-7379393-3-7

First Published April 2023

For inquiries and bulk orders, please email:
indieearthbooks@gmail.com

Printed in the United States of America   1 2 3 4 5 6 7 8 9

Also available in Paperback:
978-1-7379393-4-4

Indie Earth Publishing Inc.
| Miami, FL |

www.indieearthbooks.com

INDIE EARTH
PUBLISHING

transcend

Catalina Prieto

aim to sustain
the divine power you hold
foster the pastures of your mind
until they are cultivated
and capable of having others reside in it
once again

transcend

I. clear skies... 9

II. clouds... 27

III. storm... 51

IV. clarity... 79

"transcend" is dedicated to anyone going through heartbreak of any kind and in need of self-love. Consider this book a resource, one where you may read the real, unvarnished truth of attachment and leaving an unhealthy, abusive relationship. This book is intended to be a secure place for anyone who wants to feel understood. I am mindful that this is a challenging situation to be in and that it appears as though the sun will never rise. This serves as a reminder that you're heard, that you're understood, and that I have experienced something quite similar. I'm hoping "transcend" will help you on your own healing journey, through a relationship's clear skies, clouds, storms, and clarity. Here's your reminder that you will learn to fly again. You have to learn to crawl, stand up, and walk before you can learn to run.
You too, will bloom.

transcend

clear skies

transcend

as a child
I promised I would find a person
who I would spend the rest of my years with
but as a child
you are beautifully ignorant
and innocent

I underestimated the power
of loving another human
I didn't perceive
the amount of power it would have on me

it's something quite inexplicable
how it all unravels
until you look at that one person
and can't imagine living a life without them

transcend

I was 16 when I met *you*
somebody who I never imagined
would have such an impact
for the next three years of my life

from the smell on your clothes
to the way your dimples perfectly indented onto your cheeks
your contagious energy perfectly matched mine

- *you made me weak*

home was your arms, and the way they
entangled perfectly around my body
like the missing puzzle piece I never thought I needed
those arms made me feel safe
and were where my inner child felt at ease
home was the depth of your eyes
and the stories they told
when you looked deep within mine
home was your lips
and the way they comforted me when days
felt like nothing but torment
or the way they would wake me up in the morning
they helped me feel like the sun rays seeped through the clouds
even when it felt like the rain was never going to stop
home was your warmth
and the way you opened your heart
even when it had been taken for granted
home was your skin
the skin tainted by ink in which you call your temple
I was mesmerized by every imperfection it encompassed
it was the skin I could recognize with just the tips of my fingers
trailing though every inch and corner
home was no longer four walls and a ceiling

- *home was you*

Originally published in Love Letters To The 305

our gazes entangled
like the tinges of orange and yellow cast upon the sky
as the descending sun shed her light
and transformed into the moon

if you asked me to
I would've aligned the stars
in any way you liked
if I could have pulled a lasso around the moon
and brought it down to earth for you
I would've

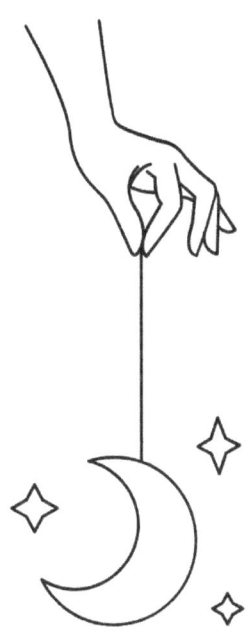

transcend

let the tip of your tongue
be the paintbrush
to the canvas of my body
and let yourself illustrate aimlessly

I am a craft
a classic painting
I allowed you to touch

- *I am art*

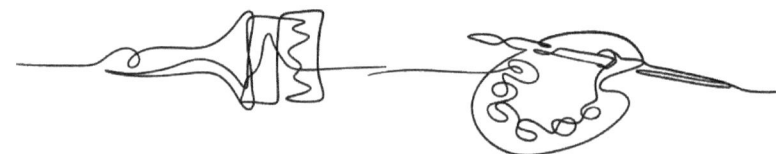

I let you kiss the parts of my body
that nobody else had
I let you discover every corner
every crevice
uncovering parts of my womanhood
that had yet not existed

transcend

you are the director of an orchestra
performing to the rhythm of my breath
you knew the choreography
to the pulsations of my heart
like the palm of your hand

I accepted you
for what you were
I didn't see your darkness or your light
your highs or lows
your thunder or clear skies
I just saw an entity
a beautiful spirit
in which I wanted to spend my entire life with

transcend

our mouths
interlocked so perfectly
they always found a way
to find you again

your rain turned my garden
into a beautiful field of roses

I watered your flowers
and you watered mine

transcend

your eyes
are a glistening ocean of honey
I could dive into forever

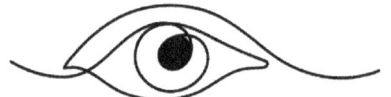

I brought my sun
into your rainy days
I shed my heat
and released my blaze
to keep you warm
from the coldness
of your life

transcend

your scent was my favorite perfume
it could almost engulf me
your respirations were my favorite melody
that I listened to through the night

you opened me up
like the pages of a book
you read my chapters
from beginning to end

transcend

like the bricks that make up a home
you kept me strong
and stopped me from falling apart

it almost felt for a second
that I couldn't stand for myself
you were always there to hold me
when my limbs grew weak
when gravity grew too strong
and the world felt as though it suffocated me
I held onto you like oxygen

- *dependence*

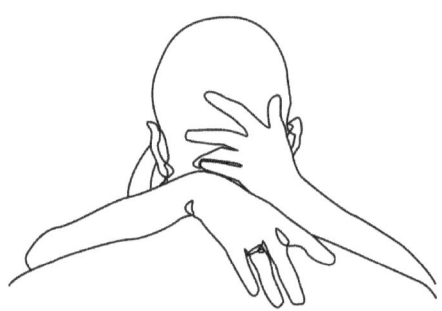

transcend

clouds

transcend

I tried
to keep myself busy
I tried
for other people to fill my cup
the way you did
they all left me *parched*

Catalina Prieto

I spent days waiting for the clouds to clear up
but no matter what
I saw the beauty in the incoming storm
I waited patiently
and yearned that one day
it would go back to what it once was

- *hope*

transcend

just because you're comfortable in a situation
doesn't mean it pertains to you

the perception you have of somebody
is a tainted sight
enveloped by a lasso of emotion and attraction
they are not that person
they are the image you've made them out to be

- blind

I crave the nights
that we'd shed our clothes
and unify
to become one

transcend

my mind
is an airplane
that doesn't know where to land
I have lost the coordinates
to guide me back home

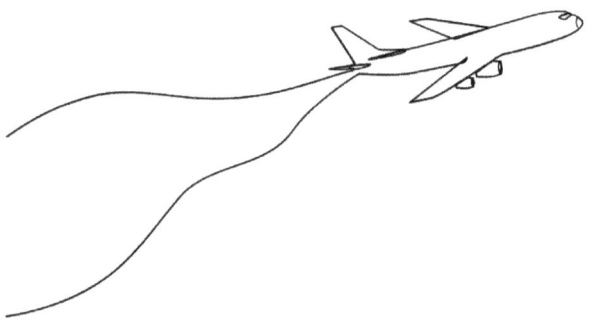

you see
the mind and the heart will often pull you
in different directions
although my brain was telling me to push you away
my heart begged for you to stay
she found every reason to keep you close
despite knowing how broken it may leave her

transcend

I don't blame you for showing me
the love you think I deserved
after all
that's what you knew it to be
I couldn't force something out of you
that didn't arise naturally
but I do resent you for making me believe
that all you gave me
is what I deserved

- *settling*

whispers became screams
compliments became insults
and compassion became abuse
we knew how bad it became
but we still chose to remain
and that is something
we couldn't sustain

transcend

the world we created
slowly disintegrated
and the future we hoped for
became a little less clear
the home that I made in your arms
didn't feel so safe anymore

why are you begging
for someone to stay in your life
why are you waiting
for someone to choose you
why do you measure your self-worth
based on their validation

- *questions I wish I asked myself*

transcend

I can't quite remember
the moment I began to change
what I do remember is
my relationships started to shift
my gaze began to dim
and my smile faded
people asked
are you alright
and no
I was tired
I was drained
I was lost
but it was okay
because I was comfortable
it was okay
because he loved me
right?

the space they left
will not be replaced by anyone else
you will not find
the relationship you had with that person
in someone else

however
that doesn't mean
that you won't find someone
who ignites an even brighter fire
within you
that doesn't mean
that you won't find a way
to fill that space
on your own

- *self-love*

transcend

once you cross
that fine line
of disrespect
it's oftentimes difficult
to revert back
to what it originally was

yelling isn't love
manipulation isn't love
lying isn't love
victimization isn't love
don't tell me
what you did was out of love

it's *spite*
it's *hatred*
it's *belittling*

- *don't confuse them for each other*

sex is one of the most powerful ensembles
humans can take part in
led by two actors
it is a choreography of movements
and an orchestra
playing to feelings of delight

sex is the gateway to life
it brought upon
our doctors
our musicians
our criminals
or the chef at your favorite restaurant
sex creates
yet destroys
it unites
yet separates
sex is what made the people
who have permanently left a mark
on your life

- *bond*

transcend

I'm starting to believe
that if you truly loved me unconditionally
there would have never been a doubt in my head
that said otherwise

maybe if I try harder
to make you happy
maybe you'll want to stay

- *strings attached*

if ignorance is bliss
why do we always seek the unknown
why do we crave
to know the things that may harm us

transcend

when mending your wounds:

1) let yourself feel. no amount of distractions will help you escape what needs to be fixed. be alone for a while. let the pain sink in until, one day, it won't hurt anymore.
2) allow love to come your way. let your friends and family lend you the remedy to a broken heart. they contain the recipe that will allow you to put your pieces together.
3) rewire your brain. meet people that will offer a new and beautiful perspective of life. focus on conquering a goal. set your mind on a new vision.
4) inhale.
5) exhale.
6) don't forget to nourish your body.
7) try a new hobby. express yourself creatively. journal how you feel. learn how to paint. buy a camera and take pictures. start focusing on this fine and detailed world we live in.
8) listen to music. whatever you're feeling, play it. whether that be sad or happy. music touches upon our souls. it connects us all. the artist has felt what you are feeling. other listeners have also felt the same.
9) *you* are your salvation.
10) don't look back. fly as far as your wings can take you. run as far as your legs can before they grow weary.

I gave you
a chisel and mallet
and you carved me
in the worst possible ways

you let my blueprint
fall into flames
and convert into ash
and now
I don't know
how to start all over again

transcend

my life was a straight line
until we crossed paths
then my line
didn't know whether to go left
or to go right
up or down

- *disoriented*

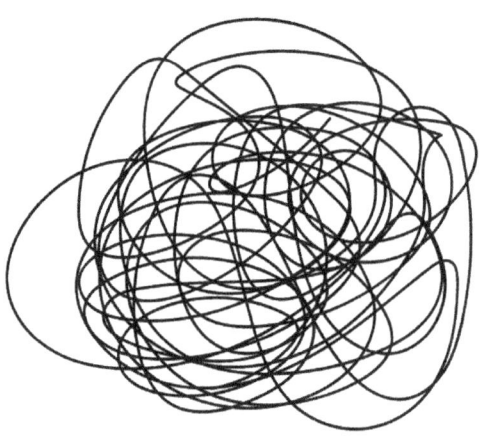

the world
drained itself from its color
and no light
could replace the one
you dimmed

everything just seems
a little grayer

- *bleak*

transcend

our spark
created a mighty fire
every time we met
the flame would revive
and burn the entire house down

you made me feel
so silent
my lips learned to be sealed
once you spoke
you made me feel
so little
I feared that one day
you'd accidentally step on me

transcend

storm

transcend

it hurts to admit
that sometimes the person we are with
is our greatest fallback
it hurts to see
that we could not reach our greatest potential
until they left
it's difficult for us
to have something we know we can't
or shouldn't have
they are not our solution
we are

I want to undress your scent
off my body
and rid the places
your hands have touched

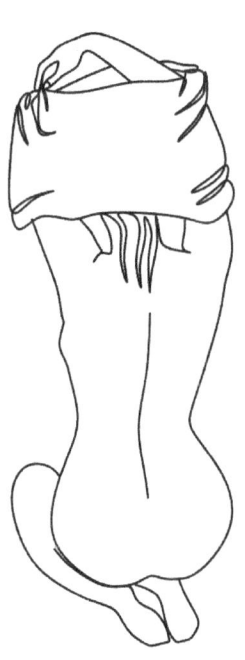

transcend

my body
is not your temporary space
to occupy

Catalina Prieto

do you really believe
it would hurt this much
if you were with the right person

transcend

you are my storm
and my clear skies
all at once

you've made yourself a home in my mind
get out
I said
you're not welcome here anymore

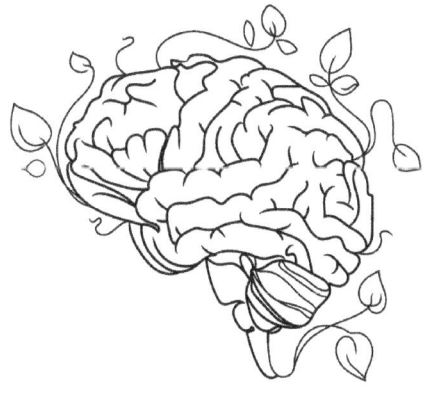

transcend

it was a Tuesday afternoon
we both had gotten home from work
the evening golden glow
sunk into our tiny apartment
the dew reflecting
upon the plants sitting in our balcony
sprawled upon our bed
we reminisced for hours
we had finally achieved our dreams
we finally had the life we wanted
from being hundreds of miles away
to inches apart
there was nothing more we could wish for
your palm rested on my stomach
we planned a family
our lips interlocked
and you lounged out of bed to make us dinner
my eyelids fluttered
but this time
I'm lying alone in my bed
your contact no longer exists
on my device
and we are once again
hundreds of miles apart

- *just another dream*

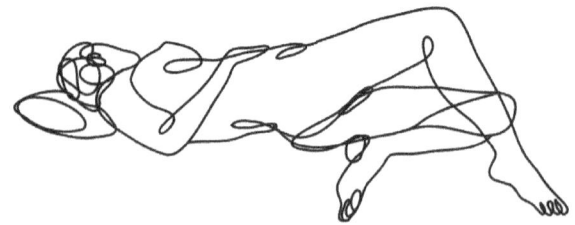

you stripped me
of my vocal cords
you left me mute
but you cannot
silence my writings
this is the most free
I've ever been

my journal
and pencil
are the ingredients
to my art

- *poetry*

transcend

we tend to lose
a sense of who we are
during the separation
of a relationship
because not only do they leave
but they take a huge part of you with them

you spend so much time
with this person
that you may start to copy
their mannerisms
their sayings
your personalities somewhat
begin to blend
that's why sometimes
one may feel lost
after the loss of a partner
one may not recall
who they were
without them

Catalina Prieto

I was the delicate crystal
that you did not know
how to care for
you had my heart in your hands
and you let it fall
you tried to save it
and pick up the parts of me left
but you cannot put a broken vase back together
and still say it looks the same

transcend

it's strange
how there's a hole in my soul
that longs for you
but it longs more not for what you are
but for the image I created of you

Catalina Prieto

you threw me into the water
without anything to cling to
you took my light with you
and didn't think twice to give it back

transcend

do you not see
that I was the flower
you often didn't water
and other times watered too much
you didn't appreciate the colors I gave you
if you did
you wouldn't have looked for another garden of flowers
you wouldn't have let my leaves rot
or overflown my pot
and then ask why I was no longer the same

we were
in the eye of the storm
the water was
oh so tranquil
yet chaos lurked
around us

transcend

I was the artist
to the painting I made of you in my head

I gave you a rib
exposed my heart
I have never been
so *vulnerable*

transcend

when you told me
that you were starting with someone else
I couldn't help but wonder
if you were doing the same thing to her
that you did to me
I wondered
if she knew
that you were still keeping me around

did you tell her
that you called me
and told me to pass by
or are you
repeating the same cycles
from when we first started

- you don't change

you are not a bad person
for hurting someone
because you were in pain
our internal sufferings
tend to lash out on the world
oftentimes
we need to get to the source
and ask ourselves
what is causing us
to change so drastically
and if it's a person
causing this shift
why do you keep
holding on

transcend

I've heard
that I think too much
that I see too deeply into things
and honestly
I see that as a compliment

to the woman who created my heart
and who is now helping me mend it
thank you
for stitching the wings back onto my back
thank you
for helping me learn
how to fly again

- *mother*

transcend

I am tied to the past
yet reaching towards the future
I can never see
where I stand presently

- *focus*

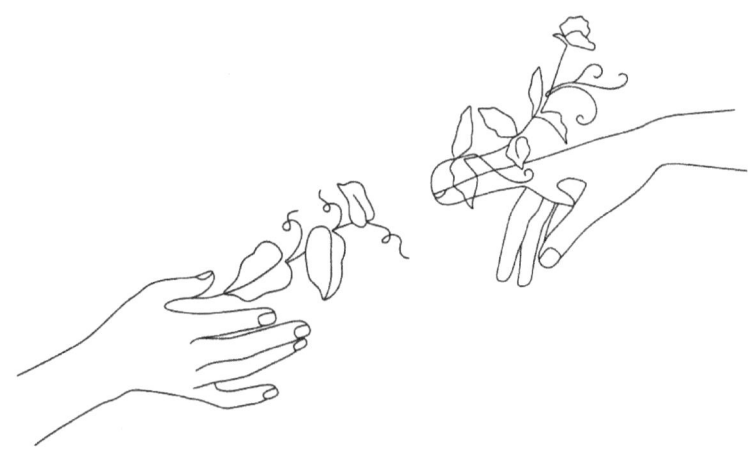

I am currently
resting within a cocoon
waiting to revive my strength
I'm waiting for the day
that my wings will sprout
and that my colors will once again
glisten upon my skin

- *butterfly*

transcend

I feel our memories
wilting away in your mind
and I see myself
stuck in a relationship
that doesn't exist anymore

- *growing apart*

there is nothing more powerful
than silence
between two people
who once begged for each other's love
there is nothing more profound
than the attachment between two entities
attachment resembles a knot
incapable of being untied
often confused for feelings of love

we couldn't find the way to unhook this connection
we feared being incapable of finding this again
comfortability is often preferred
over satisfaction
but the truth is
how will you know
if you never *surrender*
love won't pay you a visit
until you give it permission

when you're ready
let it come to you
accept the love
you know you desire

transcend

some days
my body still caves into itself
it wants to sink into bed and
I want to wrap myself into the sheets
in hopes that one day
I'll arise
in hopes that one day
I won't feel so *heavy*
anymore

I latched onto a rope
that was burning my palms
I sat through a never-ending storm
with hope that one day
it would stop pouring
and light
would once again
seep through the darkness
that neighbored us

- *I can't let go*

transcend

clarity

give yourself time
to hurt
allow yourself to feel what you just went through
show yourself the love and care
you want others to demonstrate in return

kiss your wounds
until they have healed

allow the rain
to seep into the crevices of your scars
nurture your seeds
and allow yourself to blossom

- bloom

Catalina Prieto

they tell me I deserve better
I dislike the mindset of my generation
that there's always other people out there
that if one love fails you
another will eventually come along
but here's the thing
there will always be something better
somebody who will listen to you more
somebody who will understand you better
somebody who will show you a soft, gentle love
but that deep, human connection you experience
with that one individual
where your souls collide
and your auras intertwine
that is not something you can find in just anybody
who will simply treat you better
it's more complicated than that

- what they don't understand

*Originally published in Love Letters To The 305

transcend

once your anger subsides
and you learn to accept that things
will never go back to what they were
is when you'll feel the storm
clear from your mind

traveling
is the remedy
for a broken soul
see the world
for what it is
and not for the situation
you are in

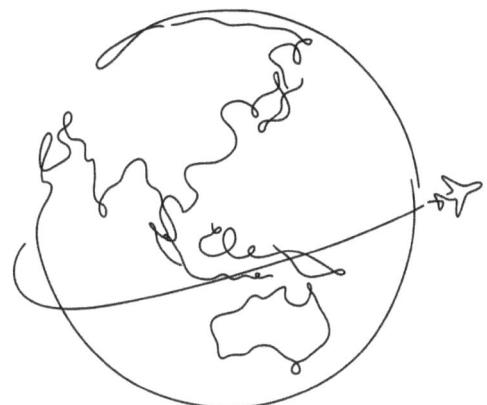

different people
around the world
will offer you insight
and a new outlook
on life
they will tap into
the things you already know
but have not yet discovered

I have seen so many versions of you
and I can't wait to see which one
you grow into next

I feel close to you
just by knowing
we are under the same moon
the same stars
and the same sky

- *connected*

the thing with love that we often don't realize
is that it doesn't die
it transforms
it transcends beyond what we know
and becomes something magnificent

the years I spent with them
I spent them learning
we spent them growing together
and now apart
I could not be more grateful
to have been a part of that section of their story

transcend

a relationship isn't healthy
when you have long periods of rain
and short periods of light
it's not healthy
when you start to feel grateful
in the rare moments
that the sun comes out

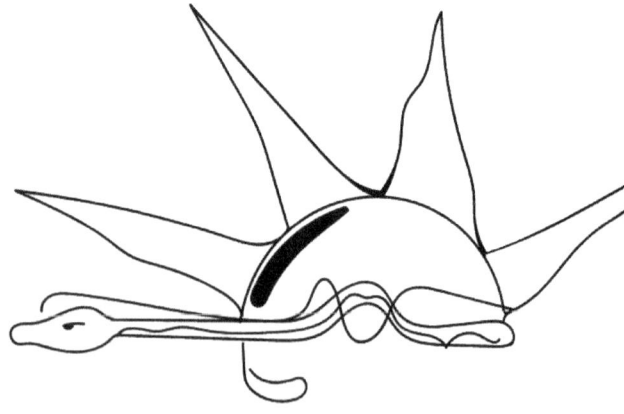

Catalina Prieto

I can admit
that I miss your presence at times
but I can not admit
that I see myself being in the same situation
ever again

transcend

I know you may never
go back to the way you were before
you were shattered
but put your pieces together
and wear them shamelessly
let them mark your skin
to show others
what you've learned

let yourself feel proud
for how hard you were able to love
let yourself feel proud
for the strength your heart contains
you were able to give your entire self
to another human being
you peeled back your layers
and showed your most authentic self

it's difficult to imagine yourself
opening up to another person again
it's hard to envision a future
that you did not construct in your mind
but you have the power to make a new reality
you can deconstruct
and make something new
and beautiful
rewrite the story you've created
illustrate a new beginning

- *rewire*

transcend

I think I'm learning to accept
that you're not coming back
and that's okay

my maturation has led me to realize
that just because two people love each other
doesn't necessarily mean they
are meant to be

yes
I might be quiet
but what you don't know
is that I have a whole universe
of screaming voices in my head
that say more
than my mouth ever will

- *pensive*

transcend

your ego
cannot comprehend
why they treated you the way they did
you can't help but wonder
why you weren't chosen
why they couldn't respect you
the answer is that
nothing is wrong with you
you are beautifully imperfect
take these moments
and transform them into lessons
that you don't want to repeat

summer doesn't occur
without winter
there is no yin
without yang
there is no light
without darkness
there is no rainbow
without rain
just like volcano eruptions
give rise to new lands
or how forest fires
clear the landscape
and nourish the vegetation
your hurting
will allow you to one day clear your mind
from the accumulating debris
and make space for something magnificent

- *change*

transcend

what is aligned for you
will occur
just give it time

to my next love
I promise I will give you
everything that I wasn't given
I promise I will hold you
in ways I wasn't held
I promise I won't let the past
trail into our story

- I will heal

transcend

although
you were meant to only inhabit
one chapter in my life
I know that
it will never be just coincidence
that two beings
happened to stumble upon each other
at the same place
at the same time

one day
your heart will feel so full again
it will pour light
out of it

transcend

aim to sustain
the divine power you hold
foster the pastures of your mind
until they are cultivated
and capable of having others reside in it
once again

to love without attachment
is to love freely

love is not always sticking until the end
sometimes
love is leaving when you know you have to
sometimes
love is saying goodbye
even when you don't want to
sometimes
love is wanting somebody
even when they don't want you in return

transcend

thank you
for lending me your lenses
and showing me what life is
through your eyes
thank you
for allowing me to be a lesson
for you as well
thank you
for this beautiful connection
we once shared
thank you
for touching my soul
the way you did

our patch had to happen
to make me resilient
the storm
had to occur
for the sun to rise once again

transcend

acknowledgments

I want to praise my friends and family for their undeniable support during this entire journey. It has been such a lovely and enlightening journey to write my first poetry book.
Gabriela Fuentes and Valeria Abelli, two of my closest friends, deserve my gratitude for helping me regain my wholeness. By continuing to listen, to encourage me, and to make me feel normal by sharing their own experiences, they have helped me get through one of the most challenging
moments of my life. I want to thank my mother for having been not only a parent, but a role model who helped me find inspiration for my writings. I'm extremely appreciative of Flor Ana, my editor, and Indie Earth Publishing for making this dream come alive. Flor, I want to thank you for being one of the best mentors I have ever had and for being so supportive of me throughout this process. I am honored to be surrounded by such lovely individuals that motivate me to become my most magnificent and authentic self.

about the author

Catalina Prieto was born and raised in Miami, Florida, with dreams of immersing herself into the creative and artistic realm. A self-taught poet, Catalina draws inspiration from other authors and is driven to compose poetry on mental health, relationships, and self-love. Catalina believes writing is the most authentic form of self-expression, offering audiences a place to read and feel understood. Catalina made her literary debut with featured poems in *Love Letters To The 305,* a poetry and photography anthology dedicated to the city of Miami. Diving deep into her work, Catalina communicates her perspectives on life to the rest of the world and allows herself to be vulnerable in her debut poetry collection, *transcend*.

Connect with Catalina on Instagram:
@caticawrites

about the publisher

INDIE EARTH
PUBLISHING

Indie Earth Publishing is an independent, author-first co-publishing company based in Miami, FL, dedicated to giving authors and writers the creative freedom they deserve. Indie Earth combines the freedom of self-publishing with the support and backing of traditional publishing for poetry, fiction, and short story collections by providing a plethora of services meant to aid them in the book publishing experience.

With Indie Earth Publishing, you are more than just another author, you are part of the Indie Earth creative family, making a difference one book at a time.

www.indieearthbooks.com

For inquiries, please email:
indieearthbooks@gmail.com

Instagram: @indieearthbooks

www.ingramcontent.com/pod-product-compliance
Lightning Source LLC
Chambersburg PA
CBHW071359080526
44587CB00017B/3139